DEDICATION

This book is dedicated to the war correspondents of World War II. They operated in almost complete anonymity, yet their press releases played a vital role in maintaining America's morale. Like a good doctor, they had wonderful bedside manners. Even in the darkest days of the battles, their clever captions and playful photographs helped our nation hold out hope—and, sometimes, even smile.

BUDDIES

HEARTWARMING PHOTOS OF GIs AND THEIR DOGS IN WORLD WAR II

L. Douglas Keeney

Photographs Courtesy of:

The National Archives

Records of the United States Air Force

Records of the United States Coast Guard

Records of the United States Marine Corps

Records of the United States Navy

ZENITH
PRESS

First edition published in 2001. This edition first published in 2015 by Zenith Press, an imprint of Quarto Publishing Group USA Inc., 400 First Avenue North, Suite 400, Minneapolis, MN 55401 USA

The information in this book is true and complete to the best of our knowledge. All recommendations are made without any guarantee on the part of the author or Publisher, who also disclaims any liability incurred in connection with the use of this data or specific details.

We recognize, further, that some words, model names, and designations mentioned herein are the property of the trademark holder. We use them for identification purposes only. This is not an official publication.

Zenith Press titles are also available at discounts in bulk quantity for industrial or sales-promotional use. For details write to Special Sales Manager at Quarto Publishing Group USA Inc., 400 First Avenue North, Suite 400, Minneapolis, MN 55401 USA.

To find out more about our books, visit us online at www.zenithpress.com.

ISBN: 978-0-7603-4790-4

Library of Congress Cataloging-in-Publication Data

Keeney, L. Douglas.
  Buddies : heartwarming photos of GIs and their dogs in World War II / L. Douglas Keeney. -- 2nd edition.
      pages cm
  Original edition has subtitle: men, dogs, and World War II.
  ISBN 978-0-7603-4790-4
  1. United States--Armed Forces--Mascots--Pictorial works. 2. Dogs--War use--Pictorial works. 3. World War, 1939-1945--United States--Pictorial works. I. Title.
  D810.A65K46 2015
  940.54'1273--dc23
                            2015006362

Acquisitions Editor: Elizabeth Demers
Project Manager: Madeleine Vasaly
Art Director: James Kegley
Cover Designer: Kent Jensen
Layout Designer: Rebecca Pagel

On the front cover: Venus, the bulldog mascot of the destroyer HMS *Vansittart,* circa 1941. *Photo by Lt. H. W. Tomlin/IWM via Getty Images*

On the frontis: Invader, the boys call him—he went ashore with his shipmates in Sicily and again at Salerno. Here Invader is shown before the big push against the French coast. Unperturbed and always ready, this shaggy LCI mascot is a coast guardsman from the tip of his nose to the end of his tail.

Printed in China

10 9 8 7 6 5 4 3 2 1

CONTENTS

B-17s line the English countryside, proof of the great manufacturing capacity of American industry. President Roosevelt called America "the great arsenal of democracy."

FOREWORD

This is a new edition of a book I did almost fifteen years ago. It reprises a collection of photography that touched a great many people, something I know firsthand because of the many letters I received when it first came out. But it's not an exact replica of that book. First, the original edition was done well before digital files were as common as they are today, and some of the photos have been lost. Second, and somewhat related to the first, when I was asked to do this edition, I decided to do one more round of research. I found several new examples of buddy photography, including some of the warmest photos yet. Finally, I have to admit it—I know so much more now than I knew then. In the ensuing years, I have written more than a dozen books, almost half of them on World War II. I have new perspectives, as you will see in the text if you have read the first edition.

This book originally came about quite by accident. While researching other photography at the National Archives for a book about the air war over Nazi Europe, I came across a small collection of mascot photography. These photos reposed in a record group that hadn't been heavily researched (which is always welcome to the writer seeking something new), but what really caught my eye was that all of these dogs were mutts. These were neither the pampered mascots of the top brass nor the war dogs so many others have written about. Rather, they were just average animals adopted in the field by an average Joe sent overseas to fight the war. They were well photographed and nicely captioned, and it struck me that this was the tip of the iceberg. Little did I know how big that iceberg would be.

Developing this collection was one of the most difficult, time-consuming tasks in my years as an author. To find things in the photographic archives of World War II, one must do it the old-fashioned way. There are no digital scans to speed through, no searchable online databases to establish a starting point. You go through filing cards with your fingers, then request a cart that comes back to you loaded with a dozen boxes holding perhaps a few hundred photographs each. You put on the mandatory white gloves and pull them out, one at a time.

I'd like to thank Kate Flaherty, a research assistant at the National Archives in College Park, Maryland, who was familiar with dog photography and who helped me sift through the holdings and focus on collections that ultimately yielded much of the material in this book. Also to Mark Forman, my digital assistant, who went to Washington to digitize the images. I also wish to thank Elizabeth Demers, who brought this book back to life, and, as always, my wife, Jill Johnson Keeney, who is the true journalist in the household.

THE TRUTH ABOUT DOGS

"The one absolutely unselfish friend that man can have in this selfish world, the one that never deserts him, the one that never proves ungrateful or treacherous, is his dog."

—*George Graham Vest*

The therapeutic value of the dog has been established beyond a shadow of scientific doubt. Well, perhaps not scientific doubt, but we all know it's true. Dogs raise our spirits, keep us mentally alert, and provide us with other emotional support. They never criticize how we dress or how often we use impolite language. When we're lonely, they give us companionship. When we're afraid, they give us courage. When we're happy, they're happy with us. They are unselfish, as George Graham Vest orated in his "man's best friend" speech. Don't ask why or how—just accept it as a gift. Our soldiers sure did.

During World War II, no one was more in tune to the truth about dogs than a soldier in a foxhole or a sailor on a ship or a marine or an airman with the enemy just over the horizon. GIs adopted dogs at every turn (cats and monkeys, too), and photographs of their friendships worked their way back home. Mascot photography, dog photography, buddy photography—call it what you will—began with a scattering of shots in the early months of the war, but as the buildup accelerated, war correspondents began to make this type of photography a routine. A B-17 crew in England rigged an oxygen mask for their dog. It was photographed. A stray dog ran through a hail of bullets up the gangplank of a coast guard landing ship in the Pacific. It was photographed. A GI was caught stuffing a dog into his duffel bag. It was photographed. Another soldier had a cat in his shirt pocket. A sailor was sewing a life vest for his dog. They were photographed, and the photographs were sent home and published in newspapers and magazines. They became part of a theme the home front needed—the boys, *our boys*, were doing all right.

The question is, how did it start?

On December 3, 1942, the public affairs office at the army base in Fort Benning, Georgia, put out a three-page press release. Considering the times, what news was important enough to justify three pages? On every front, World War II was going poorly. American soldiers had just landed in North Africa and had met fierce resistance from a battle-hardened German army. In the air over Europe, American B-17s were being decimated by German fighters. In the Pacific, the battles on Guadalcanal were swinging back and forth with no clear victor in sight.

This is Max, mascot of the 505th Parachute Infantry. Having jumped the necessary five times to qualify, Max is a full-fledged parachute trooper. Max, like all parachutists, was a volunteer.

On the home front, there were shortages, rationing was spreading, and even more soldiers were leaving home. The great "Arsenal of Democracy," as President Franklin D. Roosevelt termed it, was in high gear with not a second to be wasted. The need to feed, clothe, and equip millions of soldiers had US factories running overtime. K rations were rolling off the line at the midwestern food processors. Automobile plants were making jeeps and tanks, or bombers and fighters. Boatyards hummed with activity throughout the day, and at night they literally sparkled and winked with the hiss and pop of welding arcs. "Keep Moving—Don't Waste a Precious Minute," screamed one of the posters placed on a factory wall. Yet here it was, three pages from the public affairs office at Fort Benning, Georgia. What on Earth could be so important?

As it happened, it was a story about an army paratrooper named Max who had just completed the requisite parachute jumps to earn the most coveted of all army honors, his parachute wings. What made this story unusual was that Max was a dog.

In times of war, one must win the hearts and minds of the home front, and, along with manu-facturing, the communication arts went into high gear. Writers, designers, actors, photographers, illustrators, animators, and every manner of spe-cialist pitched in to do their part. Hollywood lu-minaries such as movie directors John Ford, John Houston, Frank Capra, and William Wyler put their shoulders to the task of producing newsreels and directing training films and documentaries, many of which went on to win Academy Awards. The Pentagon produced an in-depth series of documen-tary shorts called *Why We Fight*. With each episode, soldiers better understood why they were shipping out overseas.

Cartoonists went to war, too. Animated short-subject films, including a series that featured a character called Private Snafu, proliferated. Private Snafu taught farm-boys-turned-soldiers the truth about venereal disease and the burden of responsibility in the military, and the series even delved into such touchy subjects as morality, dating in foreign cities, conscientiousness, and other strikingly forthright topics.

But what of the fifth estate, the press corps? Despite my several years writing about World War II, I knew of no body of work that distinctly represented the output of the war correspondents, and because of that, this three-page press release caught my eye. It was common knowledge that most of the war correspondents had been brilliant publicists in their civilian careers, so it wasn't hard to imagine that they applied their instincts for a story to their wartime assignments. This press release was too well written, too well thought out, too well photographed to have been a one-shot thing. Was it possible that Max was part of something larger, a disciplined effort by the military press corps to boost morale through buddy photography? Judging from the professionalism of the Max piece, I thought I was on to something.

When I decided to go to Washington, D.C., and do some research, I quickly found that I wasn't alone in this thinking. In 1994, a junior archivist in the Still Media Records section of the National Archives in College Park, Maryland, had likewise sensed that a body of World War II material had yet to be organized. She had pursued this thread of an idea and gone so far as to assemble a small collection of soldiers and animals. The photography was striking and the situations were humorous, but her funding had been cut, so she stopped at scarcely

Above and top right: There was nothing romantic about life on the front lines. There were no reading lamps, there was no room service— just "a helmet for a pillow," a phrase war publicists frequently used. Little wonder that a mascot had such a hold on a solider, a squadron, or a company of men.

Right: Conditions were much better back on the air bases, where the front was a stationary airfield with bunks and recreation facilities. Still, war was made up of lengthy stretches of boredom punctuated by minutes of sheer terror. To fight the boredom, soldiers read.

Has anybody seen Kelly? Yeah, that's Kelly sittin' up there on the aft gun barrel. H. E. (high explosive) Kelly is the mascot of an invasion transport now helping to kick the daylights out of the Japanese in the Far Pacific. Kelly has served on two oceans and only been ashore twice in his life—on the docks of Honolulu and on the battle-scarred beach of Eniwetok. He's down on the ship's muster roll as a gunner's mate second class, promoted two jumps for his exceptional barking at Saipan.

more than thirty photographs. But what she had found encouraged me to dig deeper.

I found another collection. Yet another curator, this one back in the 1950s, had sifted through the World War II photographs of the United States Coast Guard and had separated out two boxes tightly packed with about fifty photographs each, all of them featuring dogs like Max. They were magnificent prints with captions that were clearly written for the home front. Sadly, this nameless researcher had only examined the coast guard files. Ahead of me lay the most formidable of the World War II record groups—1,200,000 photographs from the army, approximately 750,000 prints from the navy, another 500,000 from the US Army Air Forces, and more than 52,000 from the marines. I was too far along to call it quits. Over the course of the next two years, I went back and forth to Washington and went through hundreds of boxes of archival photos, each crammed with original World War II combat prints.

There they were—"buddy photographs," as I began to call them. Most of them came one by one, others in small batches of five and ten, each with the now familiar tone and manner of a pro publicist. My files grew from fifty images to one hundred, then to three hundred and more, all with a common artistic style, all captioned in a playful voice, all of them sent back to the home front and carried in the local newspapers, and now displayed here in this book.

There are three elements that make up each buddy photograph, and they are worthy of your attention. First, there is the soldier. Look at their haircuts, their tattoos, the cigarettes that dangle from their lips, the rolled-up sleeves over their biceps. Taken together, these details transport us back to the 1940s, when the Greatest Generation

Wherever they go, marines always take a mascot with them or pick one up where they are, as these two New York State marine artillerymen did. In this case, it is a little dog they found on Okinawa. They call her Geisha, and she is small enough to fit into the muzzle of a gun.

was still a ragtag collection of unremarkable young men, yet to make history.

Next, see the things around them: the tanks, the ships, the old analog instrument panels on their jeeps and airplanes with their decidedly nondigital displays. See the jungles, the mud of Europe, the interiors of buildings that now look as old-fashioned as a stone wheel.

Finally, take a close look at the mascots. Dogs have never been camera shy. In fact, whether standing on a jeep or wearing a pair of sunglasses, the buddies were hams—actors enjoying every minute of their time in front of the camera. Pardon the pun, but dogs were, well, newshounds.

Above: Marine Corps war correspondents, 1943. For a nation hungry for news about the boys, a willing corps of correspondents created a new genre of photography—buddy photos. Each photo helped tell the folks back home that their boys were still boys.

Upper right: A B-26 Marauder pilot. This was the flesh and blood of World War II.

Lower right: Tojo and his pal on shore liberty. Not all buddies were dogs. Cats, monkeys, parakeets, and even goats were pals.

Marines array their newest buddies for the press. From the left, Laddie, Big Dog, Ace, Scout, and Hans.

The captions, of course, bring it all together. Writing is a particular skill of good publicists, and they exercised all their talents here. Captions were at times whimsical and light-hearted, at other times factual, but rarely did they miss the opportunity to use a play on words or add a storyline or a plot. "Sinbad, the famous mascot of a coast guard combat cutter, is in the doghouse again," began one caption. "After a big night of shore liberty with the boys, he failed to muster and stayed in the sack in his specially made sea hammock. Sinbad is a gay blade with the ladies and, surpassing his shipmates, has several in every port."

How delightful those words are and how uplifting they must have been in the midst of a global war. Editors back home clearly agreed: one photograph won a National Press Club Award; many more were syndicated through the national wire services, spreading across the nation like a viral news story does now on the Internet. In editing captions I opted for restraint. Captions often included the actual street addresses of the soldiers, plus meaningless details about the location where the photograph was taken. I wanted to preserve the original voice without burdening the reader with meaningless distractions, some repetitions, punctuations that we no longer use today, and some needlessly offensive terms that, while in common usage in the 1940s, have fallen out of favor today. Of course, I opted to help, too: some captions made it through to their original publication without the sharp eye of an editor to clean up some obvious mistakes. That said, they will take you back to the 1940s as they did me as I first read them.

Finding these photographs was one thing; knowing what to do with them was quite another.

Above: Moving forward: Members of the Signal Corps somewhere in Australia during a trip by rail from Melbourne to Brisbane. They would join up with soldiers in the Pacific campaign.

Opposite: Franklin D. Roosevelt and his dog, Fala. FDR loved dogs, and a nation followed suit.

Before the war, Americans gave little thought to the world beyond their hometowns, but in the blink of an eye, millions of farm boys and city slickers alike were shipping out to places like Peleliu, Bastogne, Tripoli, and Malmédy. They left on destroyers, aircraft carriers, troop transports, and submarines; they were fighting in machines called P-51 Mustangs and B-17 Flying Fortresses and driving across France in Sherman tanks. But they were still the boys next door. "Millions of American men are overseas fighting the enemy," wrote one war correspondent

Above: Those military correspondents with cameras were called "combat camera." Embedded civilian correspondents in World War II traveled side by side with the marines into the combat zones and lived as their military counterparts did, much as they do today.

Opposite: Bullseye, seen at the bombardier training center, inspired perhaps by the TV series *Our Gang*. One well-composed photo such as this tugged at the heartstrings of the nation and boosted morale in the balance.

in his caption. "But if any proof were needed that they're still pretty much the same kind of fellow that left home, this photo adds a convincing touch. Dogs and boys go together—and no matter where they are, when they can, boys take their pets along." That was the magic of buddy photography: it made the world seem smaller. Displaying the images as a book recaptures that feeling.

Some technical notes are in order. The pictures in this book were taken between seventy and seventy-five years ago. Most of them were taken in a theater of combat, but some were also taken at stateside training bases. The image quality varies. While most were expertly preserved, some of the photographs have faded with time.

With a few exceptions, this book is not about "war dogs," that is, dogs trained to function in the war itself. War dogs were instrumental on the battlegrounds, particularly in the Pacific, but they've been thoroughly chronicled by other authors and, accordingly, they are not the focus here. Nonetheless, I felt compelled to include a few; when you see them, you will understand why.

Although most of the soldiers adopted dogs, dogs were rare in the Pacific. Instead, in that theater we see cats, goats, donkeys, parrots, monkeys, roosters, cheetah, frogs—and even a snake—as mascots. While many of the dogs in this book eventually became the official mascots of their units (and were duly vested with imaginative ranks and awards), this book is not about the official mascots of the various military institutions. To this I made one notable exception (and a few smaller ones). President Franklin Roosevelt was somewhat of a rock star to the men, so much so that if Roosevelt did something, they knew it was all right. Fala, his Scottish terrier, appears here.

All of the branches produced dog photography, but each was quite different in how they went about it. The Signal Corps publicists, for instance, were restrained and reserved, and almost always wrote without humor. That said, there are many fine examples of buddy photography in this record group. I recommend in particular the picture of a soldier and his dog on page 70. His tired eyes speak volumes about the misery of war, while the dog he holds so hungrily says even more about staying

Above: A good example of the power of comic relief can be found in this photo of a cat inside the small life preserver made especially for him by his marine unit.

Opposite: It's good to have a friend, it's just plain good to have a friend, or so says Soogie after three landings on his LCI.

sane amidst it all. Of the entire collection, this is my favorite.

The air force photographers, then part of the army (albeit with all the swashbuckle of a fighter-jock), were at times downright vaudevillian in their approach. Look at Boots on page 30. Or Bullseye on page 19 (inspired, no doubt, by the old television show *Our Gang*). One can't help but appreciate the antics that preceded these photos, nor stop smiling as we view them today.

The Marine Corps had some of the most unusual war pets, including a rifle-squeezing snake. That said, despite the no-nonsense, hard-nosed reputation of the Corps, they produced some of the most compassionate pictures of the lot. The marines may be the proud and the few, but they have an unflinching sense of who they are, which, in a word, is mortal. In an odd way, for all the Sturm und Drang, their photography celebrates the soldier as an individual.

Without a doubt, the coast guard had the best dog photography, the best captions, and the most varied situations. Not only did they run the Higgins boats onto the D-Day beaches at Normandy, they also escorted the convoys across the Atlantic, captained transport ships, undertook evacuations, and steered landing craft onto almost every beach that American soldiers hit in both Europe and the Pacific. Read some of the tongue-in-cheek captions—they bristle with well-timed double entendres. "Salty has been promoted to Bones First Mate," wrote one correspondent. And for the dog named Hobo, "the chow is dog-gone good."

Max, the dog that started it all for me, appears on page 8. Max jumped out of an airplane five times and did, in fact, win his parachute wings. Even the regiment's commanding officer got into the spirit and pinned Max's wings on his . . . er, chest.

While the war certainly transformed America, it didn't transform us as people. We remained a caring nation in quiet towns, praying for the safe return of our boys. We didn't hide the bitter truths of combat, but we needed good news, too. So, here they are, the good men of that great generation, the sons and fathers and husbands and brothers— our parents and grandparents. As they were back when an entire nation was consumed with the unspeakable job of fighting World War II—back when they were young and had a friend: their buddy.

ONE

DOG TAGS

MASCOTS OF THE US COAST GUARD

A common misconception holds that the United States Coast Guard's area of combat responsibility was limited to the coastal waters of the United States. Nothing could be further from the truth. US Coast Guard cutters, tenders, tugs, and transport ships—some as long as five hundred feet and manned with crews of more than two hundred men—played a vital role in virtually every theater of operation from North Africa to the remote islands of the Pacific. Coast guard cutter and boat crews, and the US Navy frigates and destroyers they manned, assisted in the invasions of North Africa and Italy and in the D-Day invasion of France. In the Pacific, they landed marines and army soldiers on the islands throughout the Central and Southwest Pacific during the drive to Japan. And, along the way, the Coasties made friends. Four-legged friends.

The coast guard war correspondents roamed their ships with cameras in hand and sent back absolute treasures on film. They snapped photos in the sickbays (coast guard transports were one of the ways home for many a wounded soldier), the mess halls, the wheelhouse, and the decks—even on the gun mounts. Like their counterparts in the air corps, Coasties couldn't resist the opportunity to outfit their dogs with props appropriate to the situation. We see dogs with kerchiefs, holding forks, even shielding their eyes with sunglasses.

The captions are amusing, fanciful, and endearing. The correspondents used frequent plays on words, accented by paws, barks, and other canine references and juxtaposed against nautical terms. Better yet, most of the captions involved a good deal of storytelling. In one caption we discover that a dog survived a ferocious gun battle with the enemy, while in another we read that a mascot escaped its German captors. Surely there are simpler ways to write a caption. But none are more heartwarming, nor more interesting, than these.

Jo Ann is always curious about the goings-on on her ship. A coiled hawser on the deck grabbed her interest . . . and then her leg. So Jo Ann just snoozed until one of her shipmates arrived to free her from her trap.

Above: Eight naval airmen and their dog Turbo are rescued after their plane crashed in the Pacific by US Coast Guard Air-Sea Rescue out of San Diego.

Opposite: Screech, puppy mascot on a cutter on convoy duty, is always ready when mess call is sounded. *The more mess the better,* thinks Screech. Here, he accepts a morsel from the tray of one of his pals, Boatswain's Mate Carmine Giangrasso. Share and share alike—eh, pal?

Sinbad is a fighting dog from a fighting ship—most of the time. When the cutter ran into a U-boat pack, depth-charged six submarines, and sank the last by ramming it, Sinbad slept through it all at his battle station—in a bunk. When the ship is in port, though, Sinbad upholds his reputation by taking on anything on paws. His five years of sea duty have made him a crafty fighter indeed.

Soogie, the mascot of a coast guard-manned LCI (landing craft, infantry) operating in French waters, has been on station a long time—three years since he came aboard in Galveston, Texas. Here he gives the photographer a grim look as he poses before the likeness of a fighting Donald Duck insignia on his ship. If Soogie looks a bit tired, it is because in late 1944, he has been a part of three invasions already—Sicily, Salerno, and Normandy. His coast guard mates gave him a rating: morale builder first class.

Coast guard fighting ships have dogs holding the important duties of mascot, but there is one ship plying the combat waters with a frisky kitten at the helm. Here she is, Midnight, in the hands of coast guardsman Elmer Barnes.

Above: Salty, mascot on an assault transport, doesn't have anybody fooled. When the bos'n pipes "all hands to swab down," the pup hops up on a boom or gun barrel to watch and bark wisecracks at his shipmates. Salty is a first-class goldbrick, but they love him anyway.

Opposite: Queenie is the mascot of a supply ship in the Pacific theater manned by the coast guard. She stands her watch at a gun station, peering through her sunglasses, ready to bark at anything arousing her suspicions. Queenie has the run of the forecastle bridge.

The brown-and-white pup under the machinist mate's right arm had the bad luck to be on the beach in Normandy as the invasion of Europe began on June 6, 1944. Bullets zinged past his floppy ears, and artillery rounds exploded all around. Cherbourg, the name given to him by his American rescuers, didn't know what to do. Then an LST (landing ship, tank) powered into the beach and lowered its ramp. As Yankee soldiers piled out, the frightened pup ran up the ramp between their legs and found refuge in the cavernous interior. From that moment on, the ship had two mascots—Cherbourg, on the left, and Boots, a German shepherd owned by one of the coast guardsmen.

Wherever you find a ship's crew, you're certain to find a mascot, and these guardsmen are no exception. Lined up for evening chow somewhere at sea, Mutt is first in line. Tongue lolling and drooling in anticipation, he stares avidly as his master's tray is piled high.

Things are just "sew, sew" at sea. A coast guardsman is a versatile chap, adept with ropes, winches, and even the needle. Here Harold Adams of New Orleans does some fancy work on a piece of canvas while the curious puppy mascot, the aptly named Nosey, climbs on his shoulder to see what is going on.

Pepper is a salty veteran of Pacific invasions. A mascot aboard a coast guard invasion transport, this frolicsome pup has barked his way through half a dozen assaults against Japanese island beaches: Tarawa, Saipan, Okinawa, Luzon. Here he is—sure enough—off the shore of Peleliu with two of his pals, Edward Lynch of Freeport, New York, and Erwin Enos of Bellmore, New York.

Mascot of a coast guard combat cutter, Sparky is ready to abandon ship if an emergency should arise. The sea dog wears a life jacket carefully tailored by his shipmates. A veteran of long service aboard this Atlantic sub hunter, Sparky knows the smell of battle and has seen an enemy sub go to the bottom.

Coast guard Lt. Cmdr. Jack Dixon was in a rescue craft as it approached a sinking ship. As he scanned the deck, he found only this forlorn puppy, apparently abandoned by the crew. As the sea rose over the gunwales and started flooding the ship, the frightened pooch climbed the stairs to save himself. Commander Dixon rescued the grateful animal, but not before taking this heart-rending picture of a sad, scared pup. This photo won first honors at a 1940s showing at the National Press Club in Washington, D.C.

His name used to be Half Hitch, but the wounded boys started calling him Doc Sunshine. Doc assigned himself to cheer-up duty in the morale-upping division aboard a transport. He strolls from bunk to bunk shaking paws and giving all the boys that "things are getting better every day" feeling.

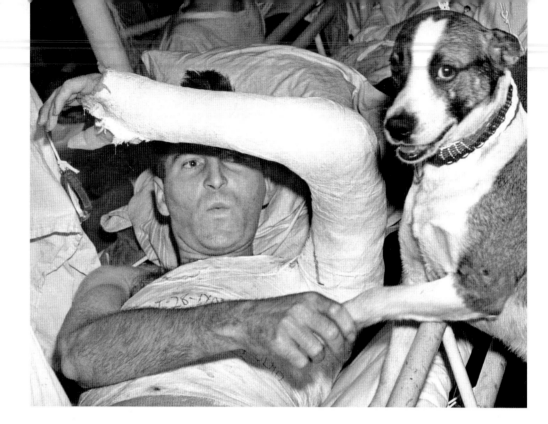

All day long, Doc Sunshine makes his rounds visiting the boys who are coming home with their arms and legs in casts and their heads in bandages. He makes them forget the war and break into smiles. Here Doc drops in on Pfc. Harold Keel of Tennessee City, Tennessee, who got in the way of some German machine-gun fire.

Doc Sunshine plays no favorites on his troop transport. He pays his respects to everybody—both the soldiers heading to Europe as reinforcements and the soldiers coming back from Europe as casualties. His headquarters is a K rations box, from which he dispenses good cheer.

Saki, a black cocker mascot of a coast guard-manned LST, was in there with his shipmates when American forces attacked and finally conquered the Japanese bastion on Biak Island in the Southwest Pacific. Here Saki is shown with one of his pals, coast guardsman Kenneth Smith, seaman first class of Clawson, Michigan, on the deck of the LST in front of an antiaircraft gun.

Right: Bunky recovers in the sickbay, a casualty of the battles on Peleliu. Mascots were no safer than the men they served—not in the heat of battle.

Opposite: Jack is lost in sleep on a cutter, somewhere in the Pacific combat area.

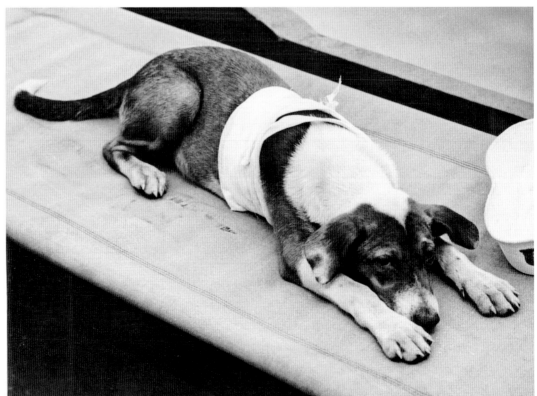

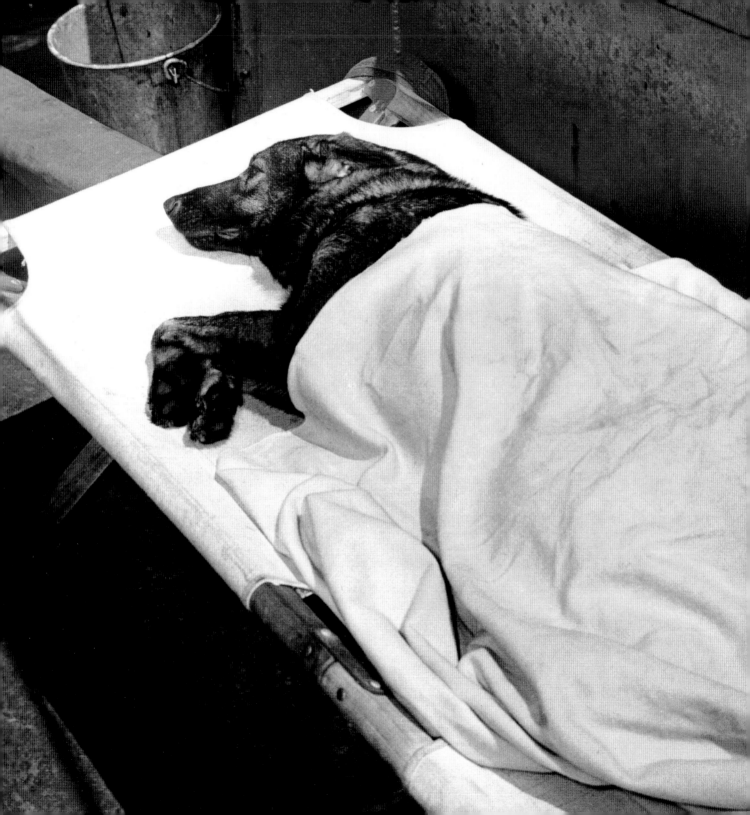

Above: Get out the Purple Heart. With a bandaged eye, Sparky returns from a Marshall Islands beach a veteran of battle and a hero of the war. Going in with the marines off an assault ship, Sparky did a good job of barking at the Japanese before an injury got him carried back to the ship. After the battle, still carrying his own rations, he swaps war stories with his buddies.

Opposite: Knobby, the mascot on an eighty-three-foot rescue cutter, found himself a part of history by being on board when the ship was among the armada that sailed across the English Channel to Normandy on D-Day, June 6, 1944. Wearing his specially made life preserver, Knobby stayed right in there barking orders as the beachhead was established and witnessed the rescue of more than 750 American and Allied invaders on that fateful day.

Above: Whether romping or snuggling, these happy mutts aboard hospital ships are just what the doctor ordered for injured American servicemen. These mascot pups brighten the day of some marines, some marked by Japanese fire, in the invasion of Peleliu.

Opposite: The boys aboard the coast guard–manned invasion transport call him Beecher for the obvious reason that he hits the beaches out there in the South Pacific. Beecher is an old campaigner who knows the scream of shot and shell and the roll of a storm-buffeted ship. Here, he conducts his own inspection of one of the transport's fire stations. Why? Ask Beecher.

Not only does Rusty Robin have his own life jacket, but he also has his own battle station aboard his coast guard combat cutter—in the skipper's shower. Rusty Robin recently returned from a two-year tour of duty on the North Atlantic, during which time he never set paw on land.

Pete the Pooch, able seaman, isn't like other dogs. He's a mooring expert in the port at Le Havre, and he knows all about military ships and the different ways to moor them. He has handled many vessels in his wartime life by jumping into the sea after the line, bringing it ashore, and then making the vessel fast.

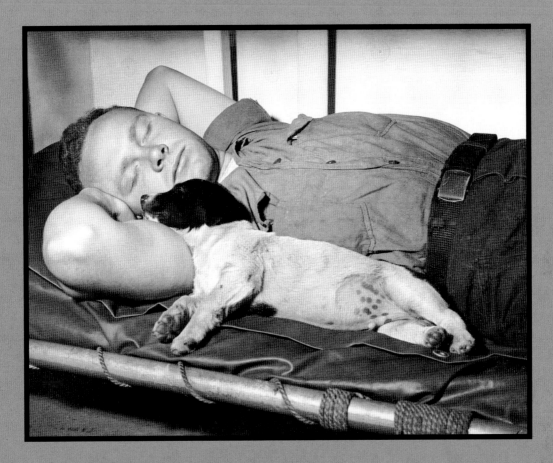

Above: A sneaky photographer caught these two buddies trying to get some sleep. Guns, the mascot on this combat cutter, and his master hit the sack together after standing a long night's watch. They were in the waters off the French Mediterranean coast where Operation Dragoon had just begun, landing ninety thousand troops between Toulon and Cannes in August 1944.

Opposite: Millions of American men are overseas fighting the enemy, but if any proof were needed that they're still pretty much the same kind of fellow who left home, this photo adds a convincing touch. Dogs and boys go together—and no matter where they are, when they can, boys take their pets along. These soldiers are part of a troop carrier force aboard a coast guard-manned troop transport in the Atlantic. They're being taken to an overseas base, where they will help ferry combat veterans home by air. You can be sure their dogs will travel with them.

When general quarters is sounded aboard this combat cutter, Sparky goes topside on the double. His battle station is flexible—he just goes where his fancy takes him.

For Irish, the fighting was about to begin. He had been the mongrel mascot of a marine company training back in the States, and when the boys were deployed overseas, they took him along. At the time this photo was taken, Irish was transferring with his company from a coast guard assault transport to an LST somewhere in the South Pacific. An assault against a Japanese-held island was about to begin. Tension on his leash indicates that Irish is eager to get down the gangway and get his paws on the beach.

Above: Always standing in line—that's the life of a coast guardsman, and Barney gets no special treatment.

Opposite: Down in the southwest Pacific, parrots vie with dogs as mascots for Uncle Sam's seafaring fighters. Here a picturesque coast guardsman, with his beard and earring, gives his hitchhiking pal Jockey a lift as he goes about his duties.

At Tarawa, coast guardsmen rescued a frightened, half-starved kitten from a shell-smashed pillbox. They brought her aboard, named her Tarawa, and installed her in the officers' quarters on the LST.

With his overseas hat perched jauntily on his head, Mike, a boxer, sits forlornly for the photographer. Somewhere in France, 1945.

TWO

DOGS AND DOGFACES

MASCOTS OF THE US ARMY

War dogs. Dalmatians. Frisky puppies, map-reading dogs, and dogs guarding the base PX. One thinks of the army as too staid and hidebound for such frivolities, but in truth these antics went over quite well, starting with the top brass. Commanding General of the Army, General George C. Marshall, was a stern, no-nonsense, disciplinarian, but he was also a morale builder who had a sixth sense about soldiers. He loved his men and they loved him back. He gave his soldiers information, he told them why America was at war, and he gave them books and movies to fill their off-duty hours. He embraced their personalities as well as their quirky fun, like dressing dogs in sunglasses and putting them on a desk. If asked about these photographs, he'd be the first to declare that the army should encourage them.

The United States Army in World War II was a global operation. US soldiers were in North Africa, Italy, Europe, and the Middle East, and on the front lines in the Pacific. Wherever they were, they were photographed. The US Army Signal Corps dates back to 1860 as the US Army's official reporters, correspondents, and photographers (now videographers). They go where soldiers go, including into combat. As a result, they have generated some of the most dramatic images of war in US history, often at great personal risk. Army photographers landed on the invasion beaches of D-Day, slogged through the jungles of the Pacific, flew on the bombers over Germany, and sailed on the ironsides of the navy. They were everywhere, and they gave us a view into the world of soldiering the way only an embedded photographer can.

Thankfully, they went out of their way to capture soldiers with their dogs, too. And their cats. And even a few other animals. The Signal Corps photographic collection at the National Archives includes some two million World War II photographs. This does not take into consideration the war photography to be found in the excellent libraries maintained by the army at their individual forts (bases) or at West Point. Ample examples were found, each showing dogs and their soldiers in situations from guarding their masters as they dozed off to providing some old-fashioned comic relief—all in the grand tradition of being man's best friend.

Induction day, Front Royal, Virginia, 1942.

Here's the mascot of the London enlisted men's Post Exchange, April 1943. His name? P.X., of course.

A Dalmatian war dog assigned to the chief of the veterinarian division during training at Camp Carson, 1943.

Corporal Satan, in Puerto Rico training, signs up for a war bond in July 1942.

At attention,
location
unknown, 1942.

Where there's a soldier, there is a dog—even if he is a bit bored.

Crouching low for maximum concealment, troops of the 89th Infantry Division, Third Army, cross the Rhine at Oberwesel, as German bullets whiz overhead. March 1945.

Infantrymen of the 26th Division wait in trucks in Ottweiler, Germany, before moving up. Technical Specialist Fourth Grade S. Mediroa holds the mascot, Little Joe.

There's nothing like a dog to weather a little mud on the way to Berlin. December 1944.

As the occupation forces move up, they leave behind a bewildering array of signs.

Recall, a German shepherd captured from the Germans at Saint-Malo when only a month old, is the pet of a US Army infantry unit near Schevenhutte, Germany. Here he hitches a ride on a jeep with Sgts. Emil Wehling, left, and Arnold Nevels. December 1944.

Company pet Leipzig was found when the soldiers entered Leipzig, Germany.

A German helmet balances on top of a uniform in a satire of the mighty German soldiers.

THREE

DOGFIGHTS

MASCOTS OF THE US ARMY AIR FORCES

There is a saying among aviators meant to contrast their attitudes with those of their comrades in the army and the navy: "Pilots have more fun." This is certainly evident in the air forces' dog photography, which mastered the art of the sight gag—probably because they weren't on the move the way the other branches were and could spend more time on the setup. Look at Boots, with his goggles and parachute, or Skippy, breathing through an oxygen mask. Yes, pilots have more fun.

By far, the two most frequent types of air forces mascot photograph were a buddy in a parachute or a buddy posed before the nose art of the airplane. Again, see Skippy but also Honey Child. This book could be filled with nothing else. Instead, I included only representative samples. You will also note that the datelines on the captions span the globe. Air force buddies were photographed in China, Italy, Europe, North Africa, and the Pacific islands.

Air force captions are sprinkled with wonderful detail and odd facts. Boots isn't just dressed for flight; we read *why* Boots was dressed up, where he went, and what he did. World War II air force captions tell a story.

One important note: the air force didn't usually identify pilots or airmen who were in active combat theaters, in case they were shot down over enemy territory where they might suffer at the hands of their captors. Who knew what foreign agent might be combing through American papers? It served no purpose to compromise a pilot's already-thin chances of escape by broadcasting how many missions he had flown or how many air-to-air kills he had achieved.

The US Army Air Corps became the US Army Air Forces in 1941, and then the US Air Force in 1947. About five hundred thousand USAAF photos are held in the National Archives, and many more are stored on the individual air bases.

Opposite: The nine crew members of the B-17 bomber *Ole Miss* pose with their mascot.

Right: Trixie is the mascot of the 16th Observation Squadron. The dog is equipped with her own parachute, which was rebuilt from a discarded flare chute by Sgt. John Patrick and the parachute riggers department.

Opposite: Trixie with her parachute deployed.

Packing for an undisclosed location to continue the fight against the Japanese, a B-24 radioman packs his bag as his two mascots give him a "What about us?" look.

Salvo belongs to a member of an Army Air Forces squadron in England. In this picture he gets ready for a jump.

Tex and Scotty, whose master handles P-47 Thunderbolts, mug it up for the camera in England. For all they care, the parachute packs could have been in Scottish plaid.

A British paratrooper and an American paratrooper with the mascot of their plane, an Icelandic dog, en route to England.

Opposite: Head-on shot of a B-24 returning from a mission over Germany.

Pinups were an essential decorating touch in any airman's quarters.

A member of the Seventh Air Force Fighter Command ground unit reads one of the pocket-edition books to while away the time aboard ship. He is en route to the beachhead on Iwo Jima. 1945.

Mascot Jerry, of a Squadron Troop Carrier Command, looks out from the pilot's position. North Africa, 1943.

When this photo first appeared in the February 1944 issue of *Air Force* magazine, the pilot's name was intentionally left out. The caption, written in the voice of the dogs, simply declares, "Take good care of yourself!"

The men of the 7th Fighter Command stop reading and decide to play some cards.

Above: Skippy, a four-year-old pit bull–pointer, is such a well-loved mascot among the bomber crews in North Africa that one of the pilots painted his picture on his Flying Fortress. He should be proud; most crews choose art of the leggy, female variety. Skippy is more than a mascot, though; he is an unofficial crew member, logging over two hundred hours of flying time, a trip across the Atlantic, and actual combat missions over Tunisia and Sicily. He has his own seat in the airplane and an oxygen mask rigged to fit his muzzle.

Opposite: A Flying Fortress puts on the dog—Skippy in the Northwest African theater.

Right: A monkey mascot perches on the spinner of a P-40 of the 16th Fighter Squadron, 51st Fighter Group, in China. 1942.

Opposite: America can thank Lt. Russell Stump, pictured here in England, for getting rid of a Nazi plane.

Major Bill "Red" Benedict and Capt. Charles Leaf are members of the Thunderbolt squadron in Italy with the Fifth Army, appearing here in a photograph used in *Yank* magazine. 1944.

Right: Lieutenant Colonel Goldenberger and his dog stand beside his plane, the *Honey Chile*, in England. 1945.

Opposite: Another Skippy. The mascot of the B-17 *Our Gang*, Skippy is one of the most pampered mascots in England. He lives the life of the 324th Bomb Squadron, 91st Bomb Group, of which his master is a member. 1945.

VEST, LIFE PRESERVER
TYPE B-3
SPEC. NO. 94-3085-8
DATE OF MFR.
CONTRACT W 535 AC 23619
CRUISERS, INC.

Brigadier General Truman Landon, commanding general, VII Bomber Command (Pacific Theater of Operations), and his female dachshund, Herman, just before taking off for new headquarters at Kwajalein in the Marshall Islands.

Stuka, the mascot of the *Memphis Belle* crew, cools off in the shade of the plane. England, 1943.

A member of the 3rd Bomb Division's 452nd Bomb Group is a veteran of the air war but draws no flight pay. Blondie is shown here with two members of her B-17 Flying Fortress, *Up'n Front*. Blondie adopted her crewmates when they were in Italy. Modifying an oxygen mask for the dog, the airmen flew her back from Italy to England, and Blondie has since made frequent Fortress flights.

Above: Jerry, bull terrier of the Second Air Force, greets Frank Sinkwich, former Georgia All-American and 1944 National League most valuable player.

Opposite: Though still a puppy, Tracer has been hanging around airplanes so long at the aerial gunnery school in Harlingen, Texas, that he doesn't mind lounging on the ammo box of a Browning machine gun. This trainee is about to fly out to gunnery practice over the Gulf of Mexico. Although Tracer has the run of the base, the brass hats never let him fly with the guys.

Above: Flash is the terrier mascot of this air wing of Harpoons flying against installations near their Aleutians base. Flash works hard at his job and goes along on all flights. Here he is seen looking things over from the lap of copilot Ensign John Yakich.

Opposite: This mascot pup greets a sub crew returning after extended patrol in enemy waters.

Snuffy, a three-month-old pet of Ensign Clifford Ramsey at Naval Air Station
Kodiak, Alaska. December 1943.

In the foreground, the crew of PCE-851 search skies for more enemy planes as
an LST burns in the background after a hit by a Japanese suicide plane.

Right: Mascot of LC-1947, Fossil works the colored signal light. Near Guam.

Below: Navy sailors gather around a drone—and a dog—named Rosie.

"Rosie"

Opposite: D-Day for Steamboat—it's bath day for this mascot of an assault transport somewhere in the Pacific. Steamboat takes his dunking under protest and wonders why his pal goes out of his way to make him miserable.

Motherly love and human sympathy are both apparent in this picture of a US Coast Guardsman binding up the leg of an injured puppy in a Far North outpost. The dogs, who do their share of work for the war effort, give the coast guardsmen companionship in the lonely Artic stations.

One pup, one shoe, one invasion beach.

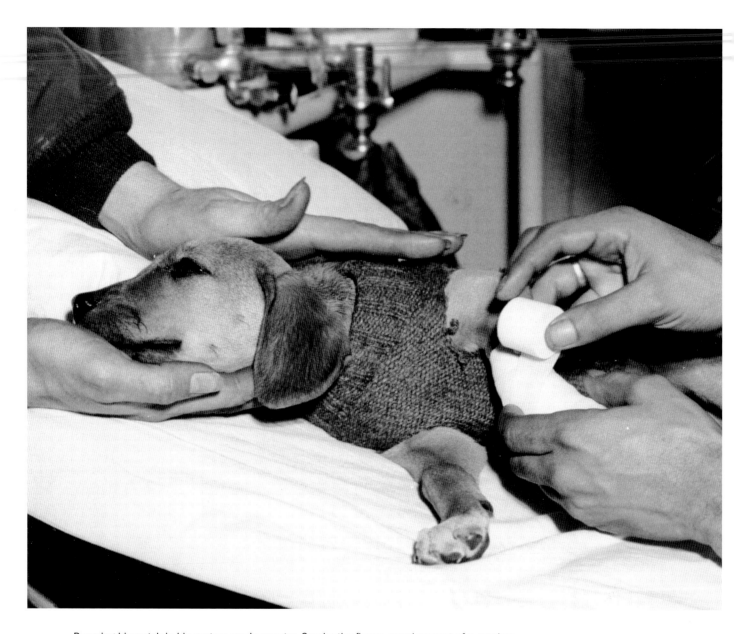

Roaming his watch in his custom-made sweater, Sparky, the floppy-eared mascot of a combat cutter, got mixed up with a high doorsill in a rough sea. With a painfully injured forepaw, Sparky limped to sickbay under his own power. A sympathetic pharmacist's mate dresses his wound, but Sparky will be a casualty for weeks.

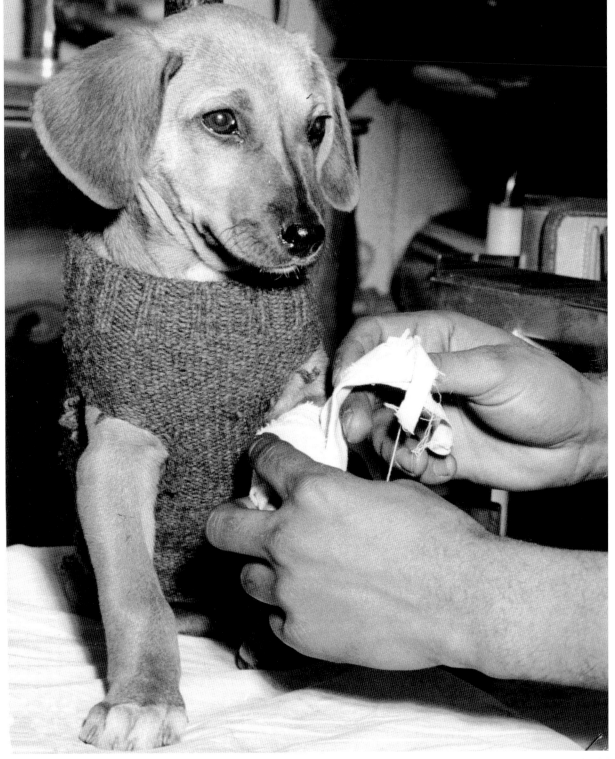

After a life of service to the guys at Hedron 12, Naval Air Station Banana River, Florida, Skippy is honored with a full military funeral and burial. His remains are placed in an empty bomb casing, which will be dropped at sea.

Mike, a mascot mutt aboard a destroyer escort in the North Atlantic, waits patiently for the word to "dig in." The napkin, of course, is phony; seagoing dogs scoff at anything as high toned as a napkin. Mike specializes in ham bones, but he'll gobble soup and the celery and yip for second helpings.

Mr. Chips was picked up by a crew member of the USS *Harris*, a navy transport, and became the ship's mascot. He participated in the attack on Attu and also has a health record, identification card, and a dog tag. Mr. Chips looks at a Japanese gas mask found on Kiska.

Lieutenant Kirk of Florida holds the ship's mascot. Seen in Hollandia.

Above: A mixed bag of soldiers and airmen spread out on the deck of a navy ship during some interisland repositioning in the Pacific theater.

Opposite: Ladies first.

Navy sailors stand in line for chow along with the ship's newest pup.

R&R somewhere in the Pacific.

FIVE

SEMPER FIDO

MASCOTS OF THE US MARINE CORPS

What sort of buddies do you find in the Pacific? Picture hot, windswept islands such as Guadalcanal, Iwo Jima, or the Marianas. Imagine swamps, poisonous snakes, and the endless miles of ocean around you. If you pictured dogs here, you'd be only partly correct. Dogs were rarer in the Pacific than in Europe; rather, parrots, roosters, donkeys, and goats were the buddies the marines adopted, and the photos of these mascots are some of the most unusual of them all.

In the aftermath of World War II, the Marine Corps did a thorough job of organizing their photographic records. The prints were collected, sorted, mounted, and boxed. They were catalogued by island: Iwo Jima, Tarawa, Guadalcanal, Okinawa, Eniwetok, and so on. In general, if an animal was in a picture, that picture was placed in a section titled "Animals." Research was a pleasure.

In the main, the marines adopted just about anything that wasn't poisonous, wouldn't bite, and could be tamed. That said, war dogs were part of their lives, too. Combat in the Pacific was an inch-by-inch, island-by-island battle against an enemy that was often burrowed into the coral or living in and fighting from a vast network of underground tunnels. War dogs sniffed them out and saved many a life. They were loved by their masters and loved their masters back. Although this book is not a history of war dogs, war dogs often became buddies, and the story of World War II buddies would be incomplete without including a few examples of these brave canine soldiers here.

Opposite: From the National Archives exhibit *War and Conflict*, a weary marine sleeps in a foxhole guarded by his trusted companion.

Banzai, a monkey pal of hospital corpsman Robert Paul, is the official greeter for the medical offices on Okinawa.

Cheewa, a small spider monkey, is pals with the marines on Okinawa. Here he hugs up against Pvt. Elwood Smith.

Corporal John Rueschlin of Paterson, New Jersey, fondles a young native goat after his return from the Saipan front lines for a rest. He participated in the taking of Mount Tapotchau. 1944.

Right: These Waterbury, Connecticut, marines are readying themselves for the next push in Cape Gloucester. With them is Zombie, a five-foot snake mascot of their platoon.

Below: Andy, a Doberman pinscher, and Private First Class Lansley of Syracuse, New York, of the 2nd Marine Raiders in Bougainville prepare to cross a road.

Above: Sack time. With a steel helmet for a pillow and the coral ground for a bed, a 6th Division marine and Friend take a well-earned rest in front of a 105-inch howitzer on Okinawa. The tired artilleryman is from Alabama. Friend is the unit mascot.

It didn't take Killer long to catch on to what's what on Okinawa. Right after the first Japanese air raid, she followed the example of her marine buddies and dug herself a foxhole.

Bowing from his perch high atop the cowling of a new F4U Corsair is Bilge,
mascot of the marines' "Flying Bulldogs" squadron. Okinawa, 1945.

Okie, monkey mascot of the officers and men of Headquarters Squadron of Marine Maj. Gen. Francis P. Mulcahy's 2nd Marine Air Wing, is shown with the NCO in charge of Okie—Marine Master Tech. Sgt. Sam B. Tarnauskas, thirty-one, of Housatonic, Massachusetts.

Bruce Rutherford's pets were born en route to Okinawa aboard ship. There are five pups in all, and their names vary as such: Nansie Shtot, Saki, Zero, Banzai, and Okinawa. Whenever Bruce comes back from the front, his pups climb all over his tank.

Buddy stands in sorrow at the grave of his master in the 5th Marine Division. Buddy has been in combat since the invasion of Iwo Jima.

Red, the big Irish setter mascot of a marine fighter squadron, mangled a mongrel dog that was the only survivor of the Japanese garrison on Vella Lavella. The Japanese dog growled at Red's pilots, so the mascot spun at him with a well-directed bite and sent him into a tailspin. Red was awarded a miniature Japanese flag to wear on his baseball cap. The pilots are members of the Flying Deuces squadron.

Frieda, raider dog of the 2nd Marines, with the tools carried by her master.

Favorite among the men, Caesar is gentle as a puppy—when not "at work." This proud German shepherd is the hero of several actions and known in the better dog circles as Caesar von Stueben. One of his handlers, Pfc. Rufus G. Mayo, Montgomery, Alabama, examines the scars on his shoulder.

Caesar posed on the beach of Empress Augusta Bay.

Safety first. A marine aboard ship en route to Okinawa with the 2nd Division is shown placing his life jacket on his "pal." A war veteran, the dog seems to accept such doings with the greatest of ease.

Now an iconic shape, Mount Suribachi rises in the distance as more marines come ashore. Iwo Jima.

SIX

JUBILEE

WAR'S END

They enlisted to fight; they fought to get home. That's how one World War II fighter ace put it. No heroes here—just get the job done and go back. When it was over, they celebrated, they sang, and then they packed their bags. Some went to their own homes; some went home with their buddies; some stayed a year to settle things down. But war's end was a magnificent moment for everyone, wherever they were. Gushed one war correspondent in his caption: "Shouting wildly with joy, these happy sailors in the Navy Yard at Pearl Harbor register their reaction to the news of war's end." There was much to do, much to think about, much joy, and celebrations galore.

Opposite: Soldiers in the European theater fire off flares to celebrate the news of the surrender of Germany.

Above: The liberation of Paris seen at night. Spotlights boldly—and proudly—light up the Arc de Triomphe.

Opposite: The war comes to an end, and the airmen sign their bomber like seniors signing their high-school yearbook. Brigadier General Robert Travis, combat wing commander, addresses the men of the 379th Bomb Group.

Above: Bringing up the rear for three marines in the streets of Okinawa is this diminutive canine captive. Abandoned when the Japanese left town, he was promptly drafted by the marines for mascot service.

Opposite: Even a dog has to cut loose. Scrappy is seen here at Pearl Harbor with a flashlight in his mouth after getting the drift of the news flash that the Japanese had accepted the Potsdam surrender terms.

Big Foot joins his mates in a little harmony. The soldiers are Flying Fortress ordnancemen, and Big Foot is known as a crooning canine.

Airmen and soldiers board transports for the flight home.

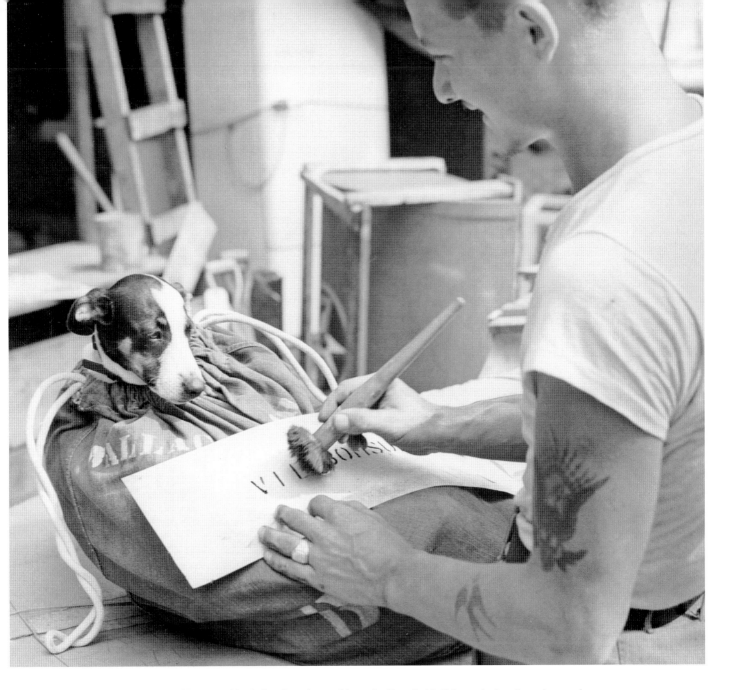

Sergeant Wallace Moore of Edenton, North Carolina, ties up his terrier, Tony, in his B barracks bag to make sure he isn't left behind. Sergeant Moore leaves nothing to chance and stencils Tony's bag carefully.

Left: The war is over, but it's back to business in some parts. Snafu, mascot of an engineer firefighting platoon in Belgium, waits at the station door for the men to return from an alarm.

Opposite: Some had to wait a year or more to go home, so they did what they could to while away the hours. This man sits on a B-29's tail in the Pacific in October 1945, one month after VJ Day.

Right: A number of joyous 2nd Division marines about to board ship after thirty months overseas are not forgotten by the famed division mascot, Eightball, who is on hand to bid them a sorrowful goodbye.

Above: Mascots often went the extra mile after the war was over. Captain Charles Eskridge introduces two war orphans to his camp's mascot, a cocker spaniel.

Opposite: American airmen, many of them former prisoners of war, board transport for the first leg of the flight home from Germany on May 7, 1945, the day before the formal surrender was signed.

SEVEN

WHO SAID I'M A DOG?

HUMOR IN THE FACE OF WAR

Being around a dog was a prime opportunity to be a little boy again, and very few soldiers—and fewer photographers—passed up that opportunity. Puppies make us smile. "Snips and snails and puppy dog tails, that's what little boys are made of," goes a well-known nursery rhyme. With their dogs, our boys were able to unwind, crack a smile, tell a joke. In this chapter you see this magic; you see this transformational power when a dog was just the right touch to drain away the stress of combat or to trigger a moment of energy during the endless hours of absolutely nothing to do. These photographs coming as they do at the end of the book, I view them as the curtain call, a fitting end. Army, air forces, navy, marines, or coast guard— when there was a soldier and a dog, a magical moment was not far away.

Oddly named given that he's a cat, but loved just the same, Butch, the unit's mascot, balances on the shoulder of Pvt. Jewell Moore, Black Rock, Arkansas. Seen in Stolberg, Germany, in November 1944.

Opposite: Soogie of the coast guard.

157

Above: Disregarding the traditional basket left on the front steps, an unknown airman has deposited eight playful puppies in the inbox of Master Sgt. G. Rushing. Little did the sergeant know that a stray had given birth under the building that houses the photo lab he runs.

Opposite: Spar, coast guard, wears dress blues before going ashore.

Left to right: Utah, D-Day, Yappey, Muff, Red, Lightning, and Blackie four days after D-Day, off the coast of France.

Talasea, a kitten pet, in the shirt of a homeward-bound marine.

Abpve: Staff Sergeant Spike eats meat loaf during a party in his honor at the end of the war.

Opposite: Barnacle Bill, somewhere in the Pacific.

Oki, Nawa, and Shima are petted and spoiled by their marines as much as a baby is spoiled by a doting grandmother.

"It's humiliatin' that's what it is. Just plain humiliatin'. Here I make the hop to England in a four-engine job, they give me the moniker 'Trans-Atlantic Topper,' and now, just like that, I'm back to primary."

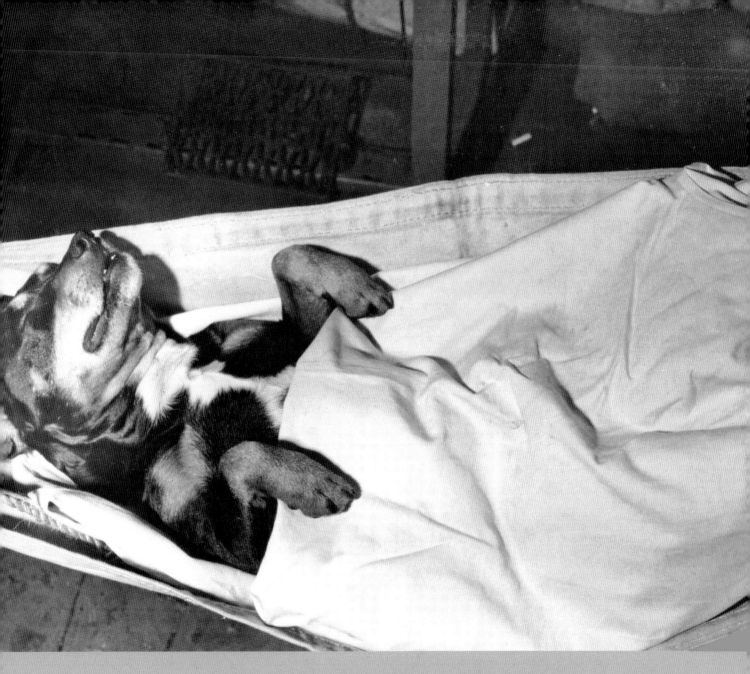

Sinbad, the famous mascot of a coast guard combat cutter, is in the doghouse again. After a big night of shore liberty with the boys, he failed to muster and stayed in the sack in in his specially made sea hammock. Sinbad is a gay blade with the ladies and, surpassing his shipmates, has several in every port.

A marine in the II Photo Division in Saipan thought this pretty well summed up how others viewed his profession.

Mike poses again for a cameraman. It's a face that only a mother could love.

Ho-hum. A goldbricker, Hobo reluctantly stirs himself from the sack.

Left: The Hula Dog King does his stuff at a USO facility in Honolulu in December 1942. All four women are part of the Hawaiian USO.

Right: Private Rusty Golding, well-known middleweight boxer from New Jersey, and Fritz, his pipe-smoking German SS police dog, attract a lot of attention at the GI rest center in Nice, France.

Opposite: Bozo watches his pals go ashore. His sad expression convinced the skipper to allow Bozo to join them.

Above: Private Peter Pelican is approached by the pharmacist mate after wounding his elongated beezer.

Opposite: The boys made sure he had everything he needed, but forgot to give him a name.

Above: It's hard to tell who is more interested in the other—man or monkey.

Opposite: A newly adopted kitten is fitted for his own flak gear.

Above: Straddling a five-hundred-pound bomb means nothing to this pilot, who is trying to play with an albatross. Seen in the Pacific. *Opposite:* Buddies. In memory of the men and women who fought World War II—and the four-legged companions that stood by their side.